21ˢᵗ
Century
Junior
Library

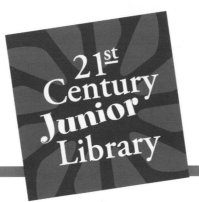

Sportsmanship

by Lucia Raatma

CHERRY LAKE PUBLISHING * ANN ARBOR, MICHIGAN

Published in the United States of America by Cherry Lake Publishing
Ann Arbor, Michigan
www.cherrylakepublishing.com

Content Adviser: David Wangaard, Executive Director, SEE: The School for Ethical Education, Milford, Connecticut

Reading Adviser: Marla Conn, ReadAbility, Inc.

Photo Credits: Cover, ©Godfer/Dreamstime.com; page 4, ©iStockphoto.com/nano; page 6, ©Cynthia Farmer/Shutterstock, Inc.; page 8, ©Marzanna Syncerz/Dreamstime.com; page 10, ©Andreas Gradin/Shutterstock, Inc.; page 12, ©PCN Photography/Alamy; page 14, ©Jstudio/Dreamstime.com; page 16, ©Karen Struthers/Shutterstock, Inc.; page 18, ©iStockphoto.com/asiseeit; page 20, ©iStockphoto.com/CEFutcher.

LIBRARY OF CONGRESS CATALOGING-IN-PUBLICATION DATA
Raatma, Lucia.
  Sportsmanship/by Lucia Raatma.
    pages cm.—(Character education) (21st century junior library)
  Includes bibliographical references and index.
  ISBN 978-1-62431-158-1 (lib. bdg.)—ISBN 978-1-62431-224-3 (e-book)—
ISBN 978-1-62431-290-8 (pbk.)
  1. Sportsmanship—Juvenile literature. I. Title.
  GV706.3.R33 2013
  175—dc23   2013004934

Cherry Lake Publishing would like to acknowledge the work of
The Partnership for 21st Century Skills.
Please visit www.p21.org *for more information.*

Printed in the United States of America
Corporate Graphics Inc.
July 2013
CLFA13

CONTENTS

You should always show good sportsmanship
when playing with your friends.

What Is Sportsmanship?

Kate was playing one-on-one basketball with her friend Elizabeth. Kate had the ball. She took a shot. The ball bounced off the rim. Elizabeth caught it. She made a perfect shot into the net.

"Good game!" Kate said. She high-fived Elizabeth.

Show good sportsmanship by respecting the other team when you play sports.

Sportsmanship means being a good sport. Doug shows that he is a good sport. He follows the rules and plays fair. He always does his best. He doesn't show off. He doesn't blame other people if his team loses a game. A good sport chooses to treat other people with **respect**.

If everyone takes turns on the playground,
everyone can have fun.

Being a Good Sport

There are many ways to be a good sport on the playground. Vanessa doesn't get mad when other kids want to play on the ride she is using. She waits her turn to play. She treats other people with kindness. She helps them if they fall down.

Don't forget to pass the ball to your teammates when you play soccer.

You can be a good sport when you play on a team, too. Rudy shares the ball with his teammates. He doesn't try to take all the shots himself. He follows the rules and does not **cheat**. Rudy also plays his best. He listens to his coach. He doesn't quit when he is losing.

Look!

Watch for examples of good sportsmanship on the playground. Do you see someone waiting for his turn on the slide? Do you see kids sharing a basketball? What other examples of sportsmanship do you see?

Listening to referees is an important part of good sportsmanship.

Good sports understand that doing their best and having fun are more important than winning. Good sports don't pout if they lose. They don't complain about calls that **referees** make. They **admit** it when they make **mistakes**.

Ask Questions!

What if you aren't sure about a game's rules? Ask your coach or teacher some questions! He or she will be happy to explain the rules. Coaches and teachers enjoy helping kids learn to play better.

If you don't use good sportsmanship, your coach might make you sit out games.

What happens if you're not a good sport? Your friends or teammates may not want to play with you. Your coach may keep you on the bench and not in the game. In fact, people may not want you on their team!

Make a Guess!

What would happen if no one ever followed the rules when they played games? How would you know who was winning or losing? Why are rules so important?

Try teaching your friends to play your favorite games.

Showing Sportsmanship

You can be a good sport in all parts of your life. Trudy works with family members. They make dinner and set the table. Don helps his younger brother Johnny learn to play sports. Maybe you are really good at a certain game. Be **patient** with someone who is just learning how to play.

Congratulate your friends and teammates when they do a good job.

You can be a good sport at school, too. Tim takes turns and is nice at recess. He invites others to join his game. Be happy for a classmate who gets a good grade on a test. Remember to thank the people who helped you if you win a game or an award.

Create!

How do you let people know when you are happy for them? A handshake or a high five is always a good choice. What are some other ideas? Make a list of things you can do to be a good sport when someone else wins.

If you are a good sport, you will be sure to have a good time!

People will respect you when you show sportsmanship. They will want to play with you. They will see that you are fair and follow the rules. You may even **inspire** others to be good sports, too!

GLOSSARY

admit (ad-MIT) to agree that something is true; to confess to something

cheat (CHEET) to act dishonestly to win a game

inspire (in-SPIRE) to encourage or influence someone to do something

mistakes (muh-STAKES) errors or misunderstandings

patient (PAY-shuhnt) able to put up with problems and delays without getting angry or upset

referees (ref-uh-REEZ) people who supervise a game and make sure the rules are followed

respect (ri-SPEKT) a sense of caring for someone else's worth; to admire or have a high opinion of someone

FIND OUT MORE

BOOKS

Binkow, Howard. *Howard B. Wigglebottom Learns About Sportsmanship: Winning Isn't Everything.* Sarasota, FL: Thunderbolt Publishing, 2011.

Sileo, Frank J. *Sally Sore Loser: A Story About Winning and Losing.* Washington, DC: Magination Press, 2013.

WEB SITES

How to Be a Good Sport
http://kidshealth.org/kid/feeling /emotion/good_sport.html
Read tips for losing gracefully and playing your best.

Kids Talk About: Coaches
http://kidshealth.org/kid/talk /kidssay/comments_coaches.html
Find out what kids have to say about coaches.

INDEX

ABOUT THE AUTHOR

Lucia Raatma has written dozens of books for young readers. They are about famous people, historical events, ways to stay safe, and other topics. She lives in Florida's Tampa Bay area with her husband and their two children.